D1505843

Fact Finders®
SERIOUSLY TRUE MYSTERIES

THE CASE OF THE

SODA EXPLOSION

and Other True Science Mysteries for You to Solve

by Darlene R. Stille

Consultant: Alec Bodzin
Associate Professor of Science Education
Lehigh University
Bethlehem, Pennsylvania

CAPSTONE PRESS
a capstone imprint

Fact Finders are published by Capstone Press,
1710 Roe Crest Drive, North Mankato, Minnesota 56003.
www.capstonepub.com

Books published by Capstone Press are manufactured with paper
containing at least 10 percent post-consumer waste.

Library of Congress Cataloging-in-Publication Data
Stille, Darlene R.
The case of the soda explosion and other true science mysteries for you to solve / by Darlene R. Stille.
p. cm.—(Fact finders. seriously true mysteries.)
Includes bibliographical references and index.
Summary: "Nonfiction science concepts are presented as mysteries for readers to solve. With the turn of a page,
readers learn how to solve the true science mystery"—Provided by publisher.
ISBN 978-1-4296-7623-6 (library binding)
1. Science—Miscellanea—Juvenile literature. I. Title.
Q163.S726 2012
500—dc23   2011033877

Editorial Credits
Jennifer Besel, editor; Tracy Davies McCabe, designer; Wanda Winch, media researcher;
    Laura Manthe, production specialist

Photo Credits
Alamy: Stock Illustrations Ltd, 18 (Dodo Bird); Capstone, 6 (illustration); Comstock Images: 14 (moon orbit); Corbis, 28 (left), Corbis: Jim Sugar, 7 (volcano); Digital Vision (Getty Images): 10; Dreamstime: Aleksander-pal Sakala, 23 (color T-Rex); iStockphoto: DNY59, 23 (newspaper), Nancy Dressel, 19 (middle), Phil Mcdonald, 14 (moon), magaliB, 22 (illustration); Photo Researchers Inc: Gary Hincks, 8 (illustration); Photodisc, 14 (earth); Shutterstock: Aaron Amat, 11 (splash), Aleksangel, 4 (btm), 29 (btm), Alex Staroseltsev, 9, Anan Kaewkhammul, 17 (paper), 18 (paper), Andrea Danti, 26 (illustration), AZP Worldwide, 13 (back), 14 (back), beboy, cover (volcano), Carsten Reisinger, 27 (flag), 28 (flag), dezignor, 19 (back), 20 (back), Dinga, 12 (back), eddtoro, cover (astronaut), Essl, 15 (right), G. Tipene, 5 (back), 6 (back), Givaga, cover (soda bottle), Goran Bogicevic, 13 (back), Igor Chekalin, 4 (back), 9 (back), 10 (back), 29 (back), irabel8, cover (ocean), Jakub Krechowica, 5 (middle), J.D.S., cover (RR sign), Jean Schweitzer, 15 (left), Jorge Moro, 27 (btm), 28 (btm), kanate, 25 (back), 26 (back), Keith Levit, 7 (back), 8 (back), Knorre, 15 (back), 16 (back), leungchopan, cover (railroad tracks), margita, 22 (btm), Micha Fleuren, 24 (skull), mikeledray, 23 (back), 24 (back), Monika Wisniewska 16, Myotis, 13 (moon), Nadi555, 7 (postcard), nuttakit, 22 (paper), oriontrail, cover (middle), Pavel Losevsky, 19 (btm), pavila, 6 (paper), Perry Correll, cover (palm tree), PhotoHouse, 21 (back), 22 (back), remik44992, 20, Rob Byron, 5 (btm), Scott Sanders, 23 (T-Rex skeleton), Sergej Khakimullin, 21, Sergey Kamshylin, 27 (back), 28 (back), Sergio33, 25, Steve Cukrov, 11 (soda bottle), Steven Wright, 17 (back), 18 (back)

Printed in the United States of America in Brainerd, Minnesota.
102011   006406BANGS12

TABLE OF
CONTENTS

SCIENCE SLEUTHS

How can lava blast out of the ocean? Can you hear sound in space? Whose bones are those? From outer space to deep underground, mysteries lurk all around. But forget the magnifying glass. A telescope and the Internet would be better tools to sleuth out the answers in this book.

BEFORE CONTINUING, PLEASE STATE THE SCIENCE DETECTIVE'S PROMISE:

I will read each one-page mystery completely. I will try to solve each mystery to the best of my ability. I will not use this book as scratch paper. I will not peek at the answer on the flip side of the page. Only after I have solved the mystery or worn down my brain trying may I turn the page.

So turn over a new leaf and get ready to solve some science mysteries.

SUDDEN STORM

June 25, 1853

Arose early and tended chickens. Sky was overcast but wind calm. In the early afternoon, the wind picked up considerably, and the air turned cold. Aside from that, the hurricane came without warning. A great wave rose from Lake Michigan up near the beach and crashed ashore. Standing in the woods on a dune, I watched the wave hit land. It was the biggest wave that ever rolled in off that lake.

AUTHENTIC OLD TIME TREASURES

Ellie,
I looked into this story. I couldn't find any reports of a hurricane on Lake Michigan.

COULD THIS STORY REALLY BE TRUE?

MAKING WAVES

To solve this mystery, you have to know how hurricanes form. Hurricanes are powerful tropical storms. They always start over warm ocean water. Warm, wet air rises from the ocean. As the air rises, it cools and forms clouds. The forming clouds give off heat that the storm uses as energy. As more air rises and cools, the storm grows and spins. When the winds in the storm reach 74 miles (119 kilometers) per hour, the storm has become a hurricane.

Lake Michigan is definitely not an ocean. In fact, this lake is only 307 miles (494 km) long and up to 118 miles (190 km) wide. The average hurricane is about 300 miles (483 km) wide. So most hurricanes would be larger than the lake itself.

Hurricane Formation

winds flow outward, allowing air to rise

humid air forms clouds

outside winds steer the storm

rising winds come up center of storm and spin

warm ocean water rises into air

A hurricane couldn't have formed in Lake Michigan. But what did the diary writer see? The writer could have been describing a *seiche*. *Seiche* is a French word that means "to sway back and forth." Storms with high winds can cause a body of water, such as Lake Michigan, to slosh back and forth. The water sloshes from shore to shore much like water in a basin. As the water sloshes, the waves grow. The waves that hit the opposite shore can be more than 10 feet (3 meters) high.

LAND OF FIRE

Marianna,
Standing on this island is just amazing. I am watching searing hot rock form new land! What's also amazing is that this island is part of the United States. In fact, I am actually in a national park. Wish you were here!
Raul

Marianna Perez

6th Straco #48

46800 Puerto Vallarta, JAL

WHERE IS RAUL?

A CRUSTY ANSWER

Raul was on a U.S. island. And the island has a national park with flows of hot rock. Where was he? He couldn't be anywhere but Volcanoes National Park in Hawaii.

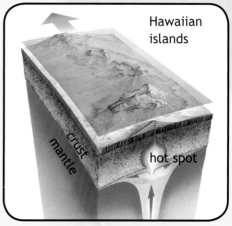

a view of Earth's layers

But what did he mean about the hot rock forming new land? The Hawaiian islands chain contains eight main and 124 tiny islands. Each island is really the top of a volcano! And new volcanic islands are still forming.

Earth is made of layers. The top layer is the crust. The crust is divided into about 20 pieces called plates. A layer of hot, melted rock called the mantle flows under the plates. The plates slowly move across the molten rock. When a plate passes over a spot where the rock is especially hot, the rock blasts up through the plate. This spewing rock is lava. As the lava cools, it forms an underwater volcanic mountain. Over time the lava builds up so high it rises above the ocean. The part above the water is a volcanic

island. Eventually, that part of the plate moves away from the "hot spot." Lava stops gushing from the volcano. But the process doesn't stop. As the plate moves, another part passes over the hot spot. A new volcanic mountain forms.

More than 70 million years ago, this process created the Hawaiian Islands. The volcano Mount Kilauea on Hawaii's big island is still erupting. But the crust that's over the hot spot is moving. Nearby, the hot spot is forming a new volcanic mountain. It will become a new island within the next 100,000 years.

Sounding Off

Space Watching

It was so cool to watch the astronauts working outside the *International Space Station* yesterday. Their space walk was streaming live on the Internet. I saw them push themselves out of the hatch and into space. I kept wondering if they were scared. I mean, without that tether they would have floated off into endless space.

They did seem to have a hard time talking to each other. Sometimes I could see their lips moving. I think they were shouting. They would have to shout in order to hear each other inside those big helmets.

What an out-of-this-world event!
Until next time …

The blog's comment thread went crazy. All the comments pointed out an error. What did the blogger have wrong?

Waves in Space

The error in the blog post is all about sound. Astronauts don't communicate by shouting to each other. Shouting wouldn't do any good. Sound—no matter how loud—can't travel in outer space.

The noises you hear actually come to your ears in the form of a wave. Sound waves must go through a solid, liquid, or gas to get from one point to another. They travel by squeezing and stretching whatever they travel through. They move kind of like a Slinky toy. Sound waves can't travel through empty space because there is nothing to stretch and squeeze.

Astronauts use radio waves to talk to each other. These waves move up and down like the waves in a rope when you shake it. Radio waves can travel through empty space. A microphone in one astronaut's helmet converts sound waves to radio waves. Then a transmitter sends the radio waves across space. A receiver in the other astronaut's helmet picks up the waves. The receiver converts radio waves back into sound waves. The sound waves then come through a speaker so the astronauts can hear each other.

Even when next to each other, astronauts can't hear each other without their radios.

SODA EXPLOSION

The family was getting ready for Grandma's birthday party. Sister set the table in the dining room. Brother carried a bottle of soda pop in from the porch. But on the way, he slipped and dropped the bottle. He didn't think to tell Sister what had happened as he placed the bottle on the table.

Sister grabbed the bottle and twisted off the cap. Like a fountain of foamy liquid, the soda gushed out. The sticky fluid soaked Sister's clothing and the newly set table. She rolled her eyes and sighed, "Why did this have to happen?"

"It's Henry's Law," replied her brother with a shrug.

WHO IS HENRY, AND WHAT DOES HIS LAW HAVE TO DO WITH ANYTHING?

HANDLING THE PRESSURE

Brother was talking about William Henry. In the early 1800s, Henry studied the behavior of gases that had been **dissolved** in liquids. His discoveries became known as Henry's Law.

Henry's Law:
*The amount of gas that dissolves in a liquid is **proportional** to the pressure of the gas above the solution.*

Here's how the law works in our bubbly beverages. Soda is made by forcing a gas called carbon dioxide to dissolve in flavored water. When the solution is put in a sealed bottle, some carbon dioxide floats to the top. Inside the bottle, the amount of the carbon dioxide in the water and the pressure of the gas at the top are proportional.

But dropping a container of soda upsets this balance. The liquid begins to spin inside the bottle. This spinning causes the pressure to lessen. The gas from the top then pushes into the liquid as bubbles. If the bottle is opened at this point, the pressure inside the bottle drops further. The bubbles explode in size and carry liquid out of the bottle and onto whoever happens to be around.

dissolve—to disappear into something else
proportional—to be correct in size or amount to something else

MOON MADNESS

The new telescope was a wonderful present for the whole family. They set the new tool up in the backyard to watch the sky. With the telescope, they could pick out many features on the Moon. As a family project, they decided to make a careful study of the Moon. They planned to watch it every night for 29 nights. On their chart, family members noted how the Moon seemed to change shape. They also noted the features they saw each night. Family members were surprised to see that their data showed the same features in the same places night after night. They concluded that the Moon is exactly the same on all sides.

IS THE FAMILY'S CONCLUSION CORRECT?

THE DARK SIDE

The surface of the Moon contains many features. There are craters, ridges, cliffs, domes, and flat areas called maria. But the Moon is not the same on all sides. The family didn't see all sides of it.

From Earth you can see only one side of the Moon. The same side always faces Earth. You see just one side because of how the Moon moves in space. The Moon completes one turn around its **axis** once every 29.5 days. While it's spinning on its axis, the Moon also **orbits** Earth. The Moon makes one complete spin around Earth every 29.5 days. That means the Moon spins at the same speed that it circles Earth. So the same side always faces our planet.

The arrows show how the same side of the Moon always faces Earth.

axis—an imaginary line through the center of an object, around which the object turns
orbit—the path an object follows as it goes around a planet

MYSTERY GUEST

I live in the crease next to your nose. I eat oils that pile up on your skin. I make a natural moisturizer to keep your skin from chapping. I have lots of relatives. More than a billion of them live with me or very close by. Some give off body odor and other bad smells. Many of us are helpful. Others are totally harmless. But I have some relatives who are real germs.

WHO AM I?

A GUEST YOU CAN'T LIVE WITHOUT

To see the guests that live all over you, you'd need a very powerful microscope. Who are these visitors? Bacteria! Bacteria are teeny, tiny **microorganisms** that live everywhere. Thousands of bacteria species live on Earth. They help make soil. They help make yogurt tangy. And they help you.

Billions of bacteria wriggle inside you all the time. Bacteria in your small intestine are making nutrients such as vitamin K. Vitamin K makes your blood clot when you have a cut. Bacteria are also helping your body digest food. Scientists have found between 300 and 500 species of good bacteria in people's guts.

Scientists study the bacteria in our bodies to fully understand what they do for us.

Almost one trillion bacteria call your skin home too. Skin bacteria crowd out harmful bacteria that could cause skin infections. They also make a moisturizer that softens skin.

Some bacteria can make you sick. Illnesses such as pneumonia or tuberculosis are caused by bacteria. But there are definitely more helpful bacteria in the world than harmful ones.

microorganism—a living thing too small to be seen without a microscope

HEARD OF THE BIRD?

March 30, 1640

It has been 97 days since our ship sailed from Rotterdam. We sailed down the coast of Africa and rounded the Cape of Good Hope. We then entered the ocean east of Africa. Some days ago, we dropped anchor off the small island of Mauritius. We delivered provisions to the Dutch settlers here. At dinner yesterday, we were offered a roasted native bird. It is the oddest bird that anyone has ever seen. It looks a bit like a very large pigeon. It has stubby little wings and cannot fly. It waddles about on short legs and pecks at things on the ground with its huge beak. One of the birds came right up to me. They have no fear of man. The birds are plentiful and easy to catch.

LESS THAN 40 YEARS LATER, VISITORS TO THE ISLAND COULD NOT FIND A TRACE OF ANY SUCH BIRD. DID THE SEA CAPTAIN MAKE UP THIS STORY?

DISAPPEARING DODOS

Strange as it seems, the story is true. The birds the Dutch captain described were real. Waddling, flightless birds called dodos once lived on the island of Mauritius. Dodos lived in the island's forests. They laid just one egg at a time in nests on the ground. They had no predators, so they didn't develop ways to protect themselves. In 1598 Dutch sailors claimed the island for the Netherlands. The Dutch settled the island and cut down the dodos' forests. The birds had nowhere to live or find food. The Dutch also brought along animals, such as cats, pigs, and rats. These foreign animals ate the dodo's eggs. Soon there weren't many baby dodos to carry on the species. By 1680 the dodo was **extinct**.

extinct—no longer living; an extinct animal is one that has died out with no more of its kind

ON A COLLISION COURSE

The audience grows tense in the darkened theater. On the screen a car and train speed toward each other. They are both just a block away from the railroad crossing. If they don't stop, there will be a horrible crash. An image flashes on the screen of the car driver's foot stomping down on the brake. Another image shows the train engineer's hand yanking back on the brake lever. The theater fills with a nerve-jangling screech of metal wheels on metal rails. The screen fills with steam, dust, smoke, and sparks. The piercing beams of the train's headlights flash into view as the locomotive hurtles through the crossing. The audience gasps. Then all goes silent. The screen goes black.

WHAT HAPPENED AT THE END OF THE MOVIE? IS THE CAR A TANGLED MASS OF METAL?

OBEY THE LAWS

The car and the train obeyed Newton's laws of motion. These laws explain how objects move. And they can help you figure out the movie's ending.

The laws of motion tell how mass, inertia, and forces affect movement. Mass is the amount of matter in an object. The more mass a moving object contains, the longer it takes to stop.

With less mass, friction can stop the car much faster than the train.

Matter has a property called inertia. Inertia means that an object will keep doing whatever it is doing unless acted on by a force. If an object is standing still, it will stay still. If it is moving, it will keep moving unless a force stops it.

And that brings us to forces. Friction is the force that usually stops a moving object. Friction is caused by one object rubbing against another. In the car and the train, brakes applied to wheels cause friction.

In the movie, if both vehicles applied friction at the same time, did they stop at the same time? No. The train contained much more mass than the car. Its brakes could not apply enough force to overcome its inertia before it reached the crossing. Fortunately, the car had less mass and could stop faster. There was no collision. Even though the train kept going, the car was able to stop.

On Empty

WARNING!

Conserve freshwater now or Earth will soon run dry!

Something's wrong with this poster. What is it?

Water, Water Everywhere

Did you catch the problem with the poster? The error is in the poster's message. Earth cannot run out of water. All the water that has ever been on Earth gets recycled over and over. The water you bathed with today may have been water dinosaurs stomped in. How is this possible? The water cycle keeps Earth wet.

The water cycle begins when the Sun's heat causes ocean water to **evaporate**. The water becomes an invisible gas called water vapor. As it rises, the vapor cools and forms droplets around dust specks in the air. Over time the droplets get bigger and form clouds. When the droplets grow heavy enough, they fall as **precipitation**. Most of the rain or snow falls into the oceans. Some falls on land or into lakes and streams. That water eventually flows back into the ocean, and the cycle starts again.

Water Cycle

precipitation

evaporation

water flows back to ocean

When water evaporates from the ocean, the salt gets left behind. Rain and snow are freshwater. You drink freshwater and use it for washing. But if the water cycle keeps Earth from running out of water, why should you conserve? Because right now freshwater is being used much faster than the water cycle can replace it.

evaporate—to change from a liquid into a vapor or a gas
precipitation—water that falls from clouds to the earth's surface

22

Field of Bones

IOWA INQUIRER

POSSIBLE DINOSAUR BONES FOUND!

Fayette County, Iowa — Amateur fossil hunters uncovered pieces of bone fossils in a cornfield in Fayette County. The fossil hunters reported that the bones were fossilized finger bones of tyrannosaurus rex. In their report the hunters noted that this dinosaur lived

an artist's idea of what T. rex may have looked like

in the Iowa cornfield during the Jurassic period. This time in Earth's history was from 200 million to 145 million years ago. The fossil hunters believe this is an important find. They have made their report available to scientists around the country. The bones are also available for inspection upon request.

No scientists contacted the fossil hunters. Why wasn't anyone eager to see the fossils?

Bad Reporting

No one called to see the bones because there were problems with the fossil hunters' report. First, tyrannosaurus rex didn't live during the Jurassic period. Scientists know that this dinosaur lived during the Cretaceous period, about 145 million to 65 million years ago.

Finding tyrannosaurus fossils in an Iowa cornfield is also unlikely. Millions of years ago, dinosaurs probably did live in what is now Iowa. But it takes special conditions to preserve dinosaur bones. The dinosaur body must be buried and covered by **sediment**. Then layers of sediment have to build up over the bones and harden into sedimentary rock. Over thousands of years, minerals in the sediment replace the bones. This process creates fossils that look like bones. Then, **erosion** must uncover the fossils. Most fossils are found in quarries, strip mines, gravel pits, riverbeds, and along lake and ocean banks. They are found in places with very few plants. Dinosaur fossils would not likely be found in fields covered with corn plants. The "fossils" the amateur fossil hunters found were more likely bones from a horse or cow.

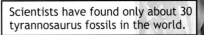

Scientists have found only about 30 tyrannosaurus fossils in the world.

sediment—bits of sand or clay carried by water or wind
erosion—the wearing away of land by water or wind

What's with Those Plants?

Green plants never move about.
They never yell or jump or shout.
They never swim like fishes do,
Or run like zebras at the zoo.
They never fly like hawks or eagles,
Or bark and bounce like little beagles.

Without those silent plants, however,
The animals and you could never
Walk, swim, or hop like a kangaroo.
What do green plants really do?

Take a Deep Breath

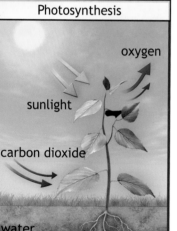

Photosynthesis

oxygen

sunlight

carbon dioxide

water

Plants are pretty. But they are more than decorations. Green plants actually make life on Earth possible. Green plants make a gas called oxygen. Without oxygen people and animals would have nothing to breathe.

The oxygen in the air is actually a waste product from green plants making their own food. Plants make food with a process called photosynthesis. It starts with chlorophyll. Chlorophyll makes plants green and also captures energy from sunlight. While the chlorophyll is drinking in sunlight, the plant's roots are drinking up water. At the same time, the leaves take in carbon dioxide from the air. Cells in the plant turn the sunlight, water, and carbon dioxide into sugar. That sugar is the plant's supper.

And here's where oxygen comes in. As it makes food, the plant releases oxygen that was in the water and carbon dioxide into the air. People and animals breathe in that oxygen and breathe out carbon dioxide. That action starts the whole cycle over again.

Science in History

Adam Smith
Rough Draft

Please check your facts before writing the final draft.
—Mrs. Myers

My report is about the American Civil War. The civil war was the country's bloodiest war. Thousands of soldiers died of their wounds. Bullets wounded many soldiers in their arms, legs, and other places. Wagons pulled by horses took the soldiers to field hospitals.

Field hospitals were near the battlefields. These hospitals were set up in tents, barns, and even under trees. Field hospitals were not very clean. The doctors were not clean, either. They did not wash their hands. They did not wash the knives or saws they used to cut off arms and legs. Germs were everywhere. Doctors gave patients penicillin to kill off germs. But thousands of soldiers died from infections after the doctors ran out of the medicine.

What facts does the student need to fix?

Mixed-up Timeline

The teacher made a good catch. Did you catch it too? The U.S. Civil War was fought between 1861 and 1865. Doctors in the field did operate in blood-stained aprons. And they rarely washed their hands or their surgical instruments. But they didn't give patients medicine to kill germs. At that time, doctors didn't know much about germs. They did not understand—or believe—that bacteria caused infections.

Penicillin wasn't discovered until 1928. Sir Alexander

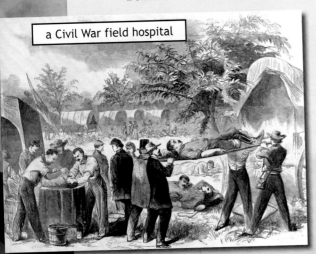

a Civil War field hospital

Fleming, a British scientist, discovered it by accident. He was growing bacteria in a laboratory dish. Somehow mold got into the dish and began to grow. Fleming saw that the mold killed the bacteria around it. He called the mold penicillin. Other scientists then began studying penicillin. They learned how to produce it in large quantities. It wasn't until 1944 that the medicine was used to treat soldiers during war.

MYSTERIES OF SCIENCE

Here's one last mystery. What do the clues describe?

1) It knows how movement happens but cannot move itself.

2) It knows whether weather will happen.

3) It knows how to wave but has never lifted a hand.

4) It knows many layers and it rocks!

THE CLUES DESCRIBE SCIENCE!

Scientists work to understand everything in our world. They are like detectives, always searching for clues to solve the next mystery. If you love mysteries too, then digging into science just might be a dream come true!

GLOSSARY

axis (AK-sis)—an imaginary line through the center of an object, around which the object turns

bacteria (bak-TEER-ee-uh)—one-celled, microscopic living things that exist all around; many bacteria are useful, but some cause disease

carbon dioxide (KAHR-buhn dy-AHK-syd)—a colorless, odorless gas that people and animals breathe out; plants take in carbon dioxide because they need it to live

dissolve (di-ZOLV)—to disappear into something else

erosion (i-ROH-zhuhn)—the wearing away of land by water or wind

evaporate (i-VA-puh-rayt)—to change from a liquid into a vapor or a gas

extinct (ik-STINGKT)—no longer living; an extinct animal is one that has died out with no more of its kind

microorganism (mye-kro-OR-gan-iz-um)—a living thing too small to be seen without a microscope

orbit (OR-bit)—the path an object follows as it goes around the Sun or a planet

precipitation (pri-sip-i-TAY-shuhn)—water that falls from clouds to the earth's surface; precipitation can be rain, hail, sleet, or snow

pressure (PRESH-ur)—a force that pushes on something

proportional (pruh-POR-shuhn-uhl)—to be correct in size or amount to something else

sediment (SED-uh-muhnt)—bits of sand or clay carried by water or wind

READ MORE

Levete, Sarah. *Science Fact or Fiction? You Decide!* Crabtree Connections. New York: Crabtree Pub., 2011.

Montgomery, Heather L. *The Case of the Missing Arctic Fox and Other True Animal Mysteries for You to Solve.* Seriously True Mysteries. Mankato, Minn.: Capstone Press., 2012.

Yoder, Eric, and Natalie Yoder. *65 Short Mysteries You Solve With Science!* One Minute Mysteries. Washington, D.C.: Science, Naturally!, 2008.

INTERNET SITES

FactHound offers a safe, fun way to find Internet sites related to this book. All of the sites on FactHound have been researched by our staff.

Here's all you do:

Visit *www.facthound.com*

Type in this code: 9781429676236

INDEX